QUIET MOMENTS for COUPLES

Compiled by

H. Norman Wright

Illustrated by

Stacie Merlo

HARVEST HOUSE PUBLISHERS
Eugene, Oregon 97402

Unless otherwise indicated, text is written by H. Norman Wright.
Artwork by Stacie Merlo.
Designed by Koechel Peterson & Associates, Minneapolis, Minnesota.

QUIET MOMENTS FOR COUPLES

Copyright © 1995 by Harvest House Publishers
Eugene, Oregon 97402

ISBN 1-56507-375-4

Printed in Mexico.

98 99 00 01 02 — 10 9 8 7 6 5 4 3

With Love To:

....

From:

....

On:

....

Quiet Moments seem so rare, so fleeting when they
do occur—but so highly desired. Such moments are a time
to reflect upon love past, love present, and love in the future.
We all need those occasional reminders of the love and passion
that caused a relationship to blossom. Upon such reminders,
feelings and desires that have diminished over the years
are given an opportunity for renewal.

As you read, do so slowly and thoughtfully.
Reflect upon your life and your relationship. Focus on
what *can* be rather than on what *may not* be. Then respond
to these words of love and reawaken your relationship.

—H. NORMAN WRIGHT

$\mathcal{T}$he most wonderful of all things
in life is realizing something special has
begun from two hearts, once joined in
friendship, uniting now in love.

The whole thing begins with a
wondrous looking, a helpless staring,
an irresistible compulsion simply to behold.
For suddenly there is so much to see! So much
is revealed when two people dare to stand in
the radiance of one another's love.

~

—MIKE MASON

I never saw so sweet a face
As that I stood before.
My heart has left its dwelling place
And can return no more.

—"FIRST LOVE," JOHN CLARE

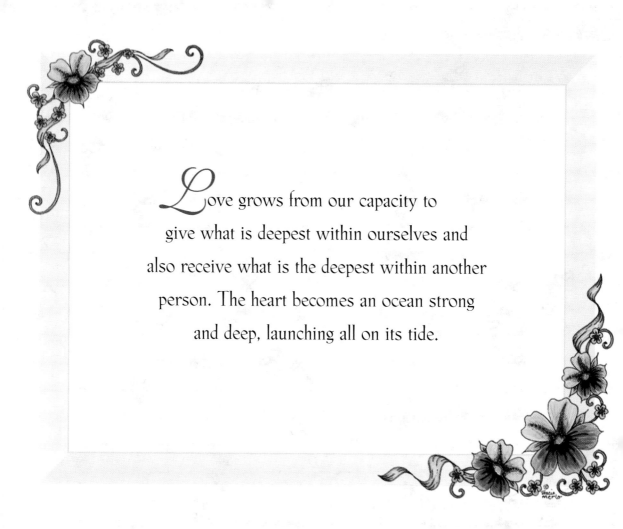

$\mathcal{L}$ove grows from our capacity to
give what is deepest within ourselves and
also receive what is the deepest within another
person. The heart becomes an ocean strong
and deep, launching all on its tide.

$\mathscr{M}$y bounty is as boundless as the sea,

My love as deep; the more I give to thee,

The more I have....

〜

—WILLIAM SHAKESPEARE

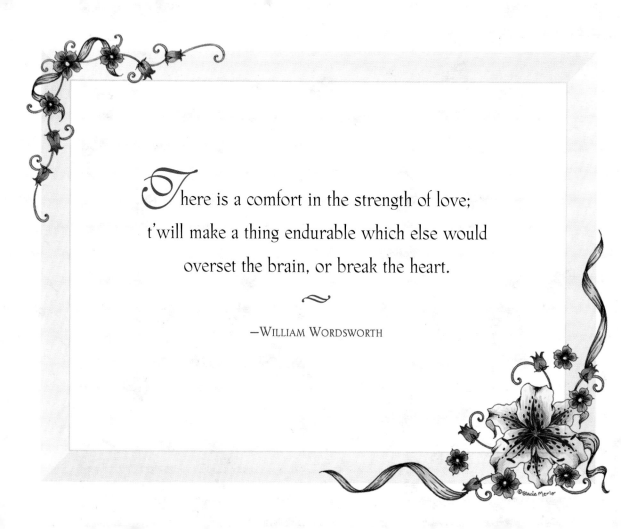

There is a comfort in the strength of love;
t'will make a thing endurable which else would
overset the brain, or break the heart.

—WILLIAM WORDSWORTH

$\mathcal{T}$is you alone that sweetens life,
and makes one wish the wings
of time were clipt.

$\sim$

—JOHN HERVEY

$\mathcal{O}$ne loving heart
sets another on fire.

—AUGUSTINE

$\mathscr{C}$ouples who love
each other tell each other a thousand
things without talking.

~

—PROVERB

$\mathscr{T}$he supreme happiness of life
is the conviction that we are loved.

~

—Victor Hugo

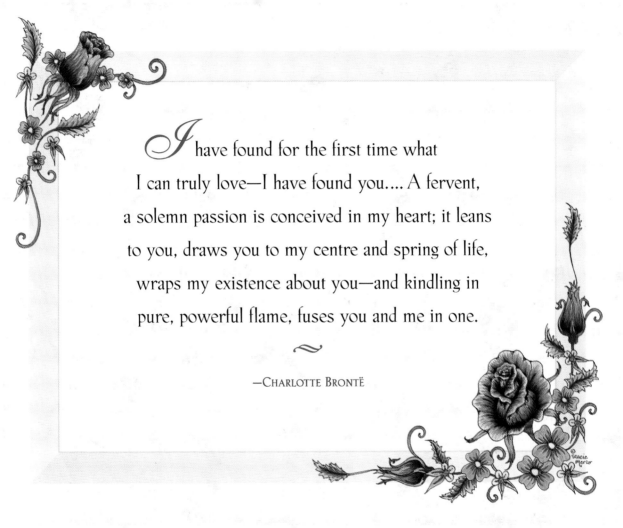

I have found for the first time what
I can truly love—I have found you.... A fervent,
a solemn passion is conceived in my heart; it leans
to you, draws you to my centre and spring of life,
wraps my existence about you—and kindling in
pure, powerful flame, fuses you and me in one.

~

—CHARLOTTE BRONTË

*F*amiliar acts are beautiful through love.

∽

—PERCY SHELLEY

HOPES ALL THINGS

$\mathcal{L}$ove is a long conversation where each
tells by gentle words, by glances, by thoughtful
deeds and unexpected kindness, that you care,
that you understand, that you will be true.

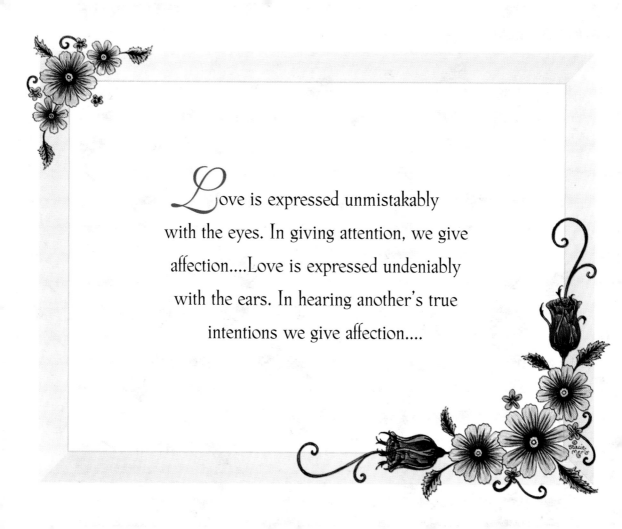

$\mathcal{L}$ove is expressed unmistakably
with the eyes. In giving attention, we give
affection....Love is expressed undeniably
with the ears. In hearing another's true
intentions we give affection....

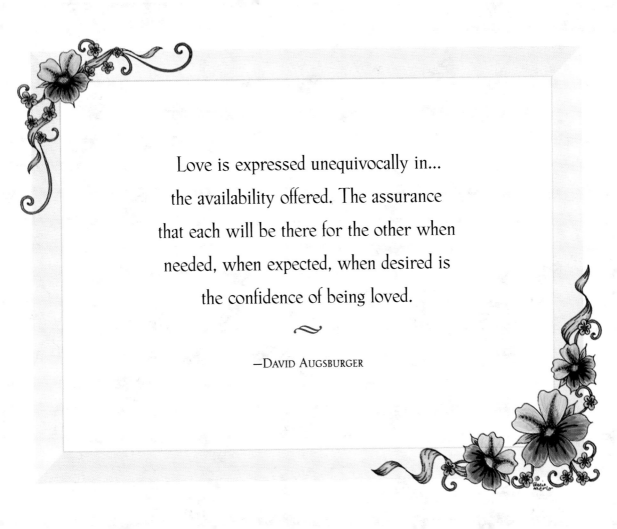

Love is expressed unequivocally in...
the availability offered. The assurance
that each will be there for the other when
needed, when expected, when desired is
the confidence of being loved.

—DAVID AUGSBURGER

$\mathcal{T}$here are times
when being called by name
is the most comforting
experience in the world.

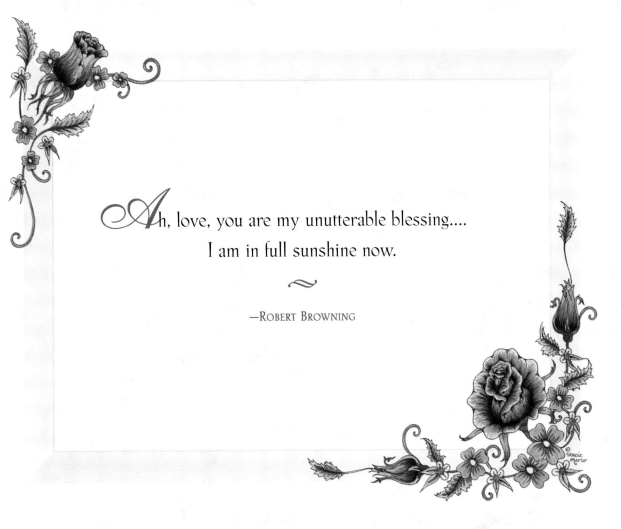

*A*h, love, you are my unutterable blessing....
I am in full sunshine now.

—Robert Browning

$\mathscr{L}$ove expands: it not only
sees more and enfolds more, it causes
its object to bloom.

~

—HUGH PRATHER

$\mathcal{I}$ love you because you are helping me to make

    Of the lumber of my life

    Not a tavern, but a temple;

    Out of the words of my everyday

    Not a reproach, but a song.

             ~

—JOAN WINMILL BROWN & BILL BROWN

 *M*any waters cannot
quench love, neither can
the floods drown it.

—Song of Solomon 8:7 (KJV)

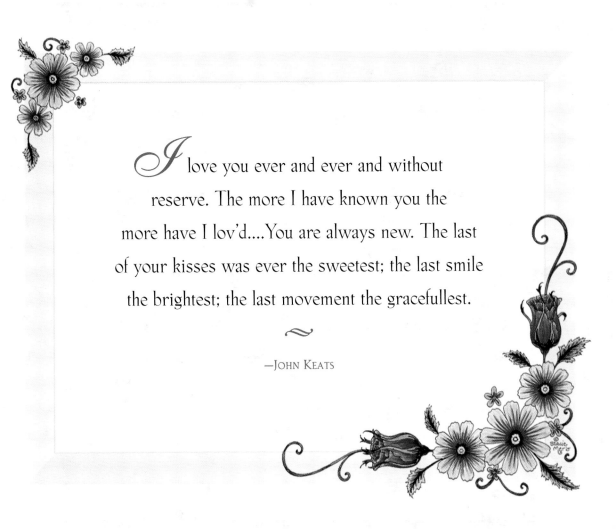

I love you ever and ever and without reserve. The more I have known you the more have I lov'd....You are always new. The last of your kisses was ever the sweetest; the last smile the brightest; the last movement the gracefullest.

❧

—JOHN KEATS

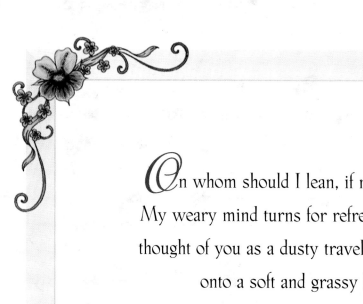

*O*n whom should I lean, if not on you?
My weary mind turns for refreshment to the
thought of you as a dusty traveller might sink
onto a soft and grassy bank.

—GUSTAVE FLAUBERT, 1853

*S*et me as a seal upon thine heart,
as a seal upon thine arm, for love is strong.

~

—SONG OF SOLOMON 8:6 (KJV)

All my soul follows
you, love—encircles you—
and I live in being yours.

—ROBERT BROWNING, 1846

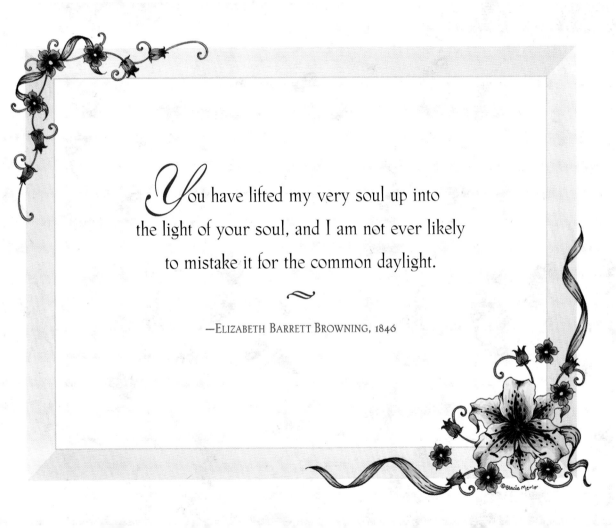

You have lifted my very soul up into
the light of your soul, and I am not ever likely
to mistake it for the common daylight.

~

—ELIZABETH BARRETT BROWNING, 1846

$\mathcal{L}$ove cannot endure indifference.
It needs to be wanted. Like a lamp, it needs to
be fed out of the oil of another's heart.

∽

—HENRY WARD BEECHER

BELIEVES ALL THINGS

$\mathcal{W}$hoso loves believes the impossible.

—Elizabeth Barrett Browning

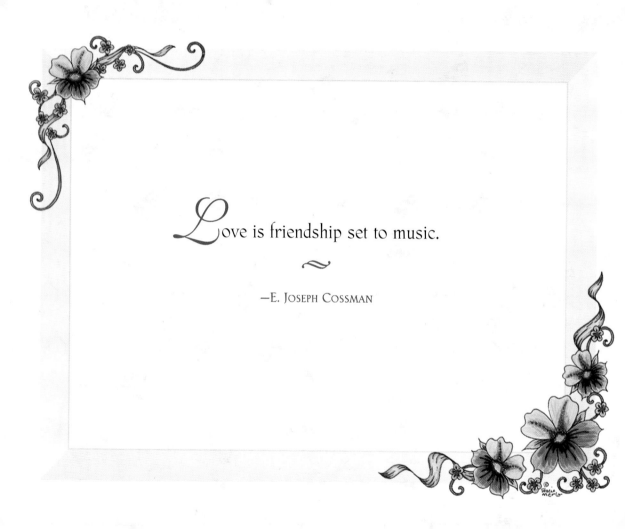

$\mathcal{L}$ove is friendship set to music.

〜

—E. JOSEPH COSSMAN

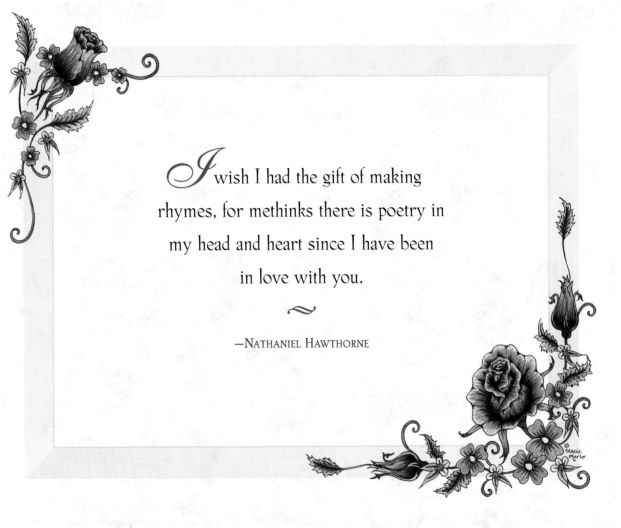

I wish I had the gift of making rhymes, for methinks there is poetry in my head and heart since I have been in love with you.

—NATHANIEL HAWTHORNE

There are quiet times of romance
and there are romantic highs during which
lovers feel alive, full of music and poetry,
and life takes on new meaning.

©Stacie Merlo

*R*omance is an attitude. It is a man and
woman being alive to one another....It is an
atmosphere—a look that speaks more eloquently than
words, a squeeze of the hand as you pass each other
in a crowded room, a pat on the head or the shoulder
for no particular reason. Romance is an element of
fascination and delight that culminates in a deep desire
to experience all of life with the one we love.

—Joan Winmill Brown & Bill Brown

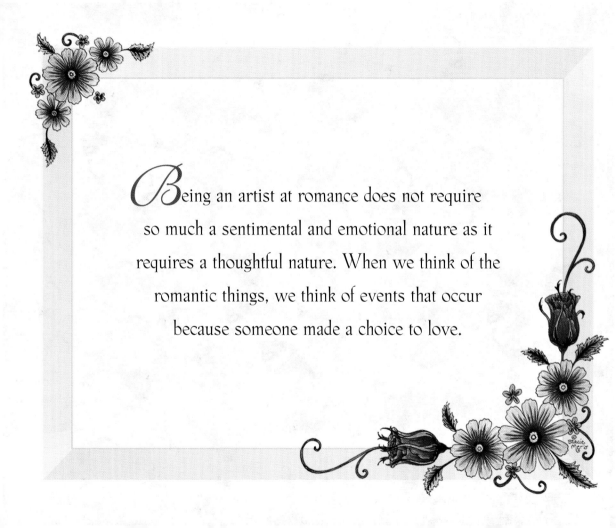

$\mathcal{B}$eing an artist at romance does not require so much a sentimental and emotional nature as it requires a thoughtful nature. When we think of the romantic things, we think of events that occur because someone made a choice to love.

A man stops off at a florist and brings his wife
a single rose in the evening, a girl makes her lover
a lemon pie with just the degree of tartness he likes,
a wife makes arrangements for her husband to take
the caribou-hunting trip he thought he'd never
afford—these are not the goo of sweet emotion,
they are the stuff that comes from resolution and
determination, and they are strong mortar.

~

—ALAN LOY MCGINNIS

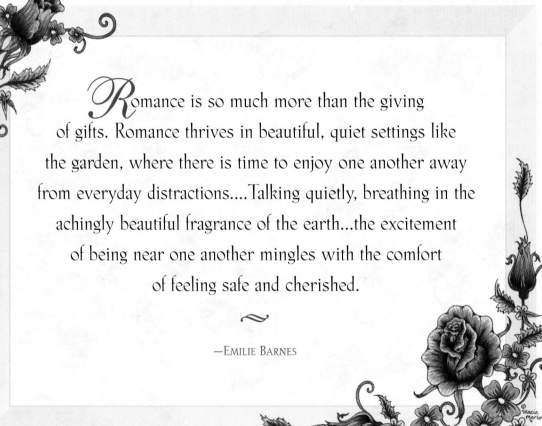

*R*omance is so much more than the giving
of gifts. Romance thrives in beautiful, quiet settings like
the garden, where there is time to enjoy one another away
from everyday distractions....Talking quietly, breathing in the
achingly beautiful fragrance of the earth...the excitement
of being near one another mingles with the comfort
of feeling safe and cherished.

—Emilie Barnes

All the beautiful sentiments in the world
weigh less than a single lovely action.

—JAMES RUSSELL LOWELL

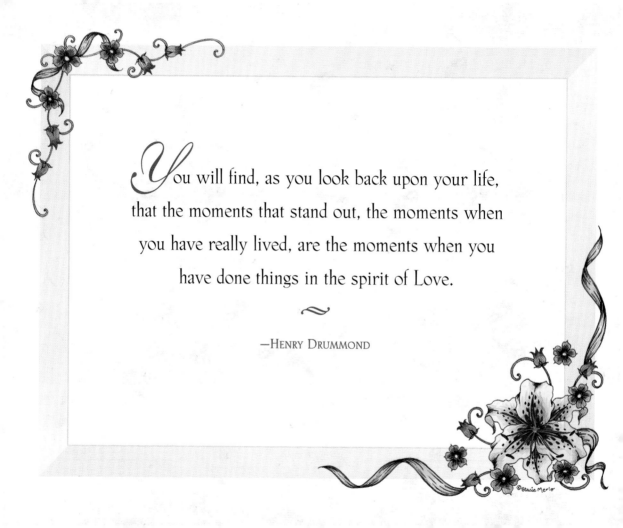

*Y*ou will find, as you look back upon your life, that the moments that stand out, the moments when you have really lived, are the moments when you have done things in the spirit of Love.

—HENRY DRUMMOND

The quiet thoughts
of two people a long time in love
touch lightly
like birds nesting in each other's warmth
you will know them by their laughter
but to each other
they speak mostly through their solitude
if they find themselves apart
they may dream of sitting undisturbed
in each other's presence
of wrapping themselves warmly
in each other's ease

—HUGH PRATHER

$\mathcal{L}$ove seeks one thing only:
the good of the one loved. It leaves
all other secondary effects to take care
of themselves. Love, therefore,
is its own reward.

~

—THOMAS MERTON

ENDURES ALL THINGS

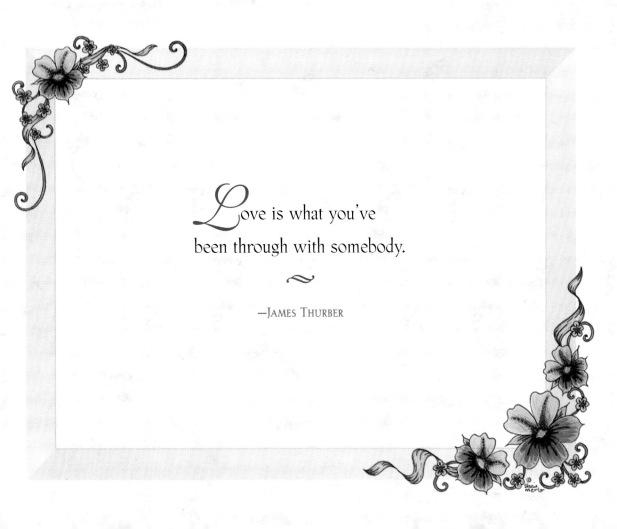

$\mathcal{L}$ove is what you've
been through with somebody.

~

—JAMES THURBER

*S*weet thoughts, kind whispers,
a listening ear, and a helping hand—
these are the things that speak your beloved's
language. No special setting can take the place
of word and deed given from the heart.

*L*ife is short and we never
have enough time for gladdening
the hearts of those who travel the way
with us. O, be swift to love!
Make haste to be kind.

~

—HENRI F. AMIEL

To renounce your individuality,
to see with another's eyes, to hear
with another's ears, to be two and yet
but one, to so melt and mingle that you no
longer know you are you or another,
to constantly absorb and constantly
radiate, to reduce earth,

sea and sky and all that is in
them to a single being so wholly that
nothing whatever is withheld, to be prepared
at any moment for sacrifice, to double your
personality in bestowing it—that is love.

—Theophile Gautier

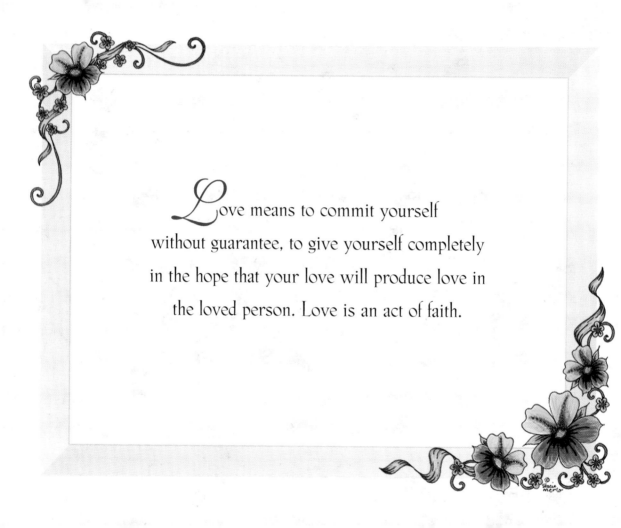

$\mathcal{L}$ove means to commit yourself
without guarantee, to give yourself completely
in the hope that your love will produce love in
the loved person. Love is an act of faith.

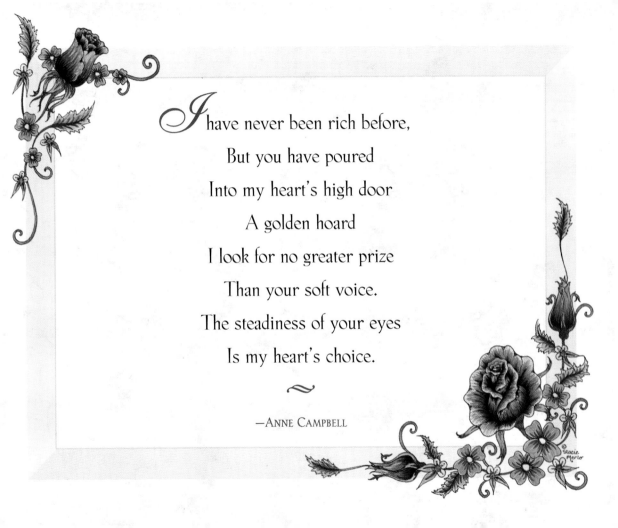

I have never been rich before,

But you have poured

Into my heart's high door

A golden hoard

I look for no greater prize

Than your soft voice.

The steadiness of your eyes

Is my heart's choice.

—ANNE CAMPBELL

$\mathscr{L}$ove has its

reasons which reason

does not understand.

—BLAISE PASCAL

My true-love hath my heart,

and I have his,

By just exchange one for the other given;

I hold his dear,

and mine he cannot miss,

There never was a better bargain driven.

~

—SIDNEY

The way to love someone is
to lightly run your finger over that person's
soul until you find a crack, and then gently
pour your love into that crack.

—Keith Miller

NEVER FAILS

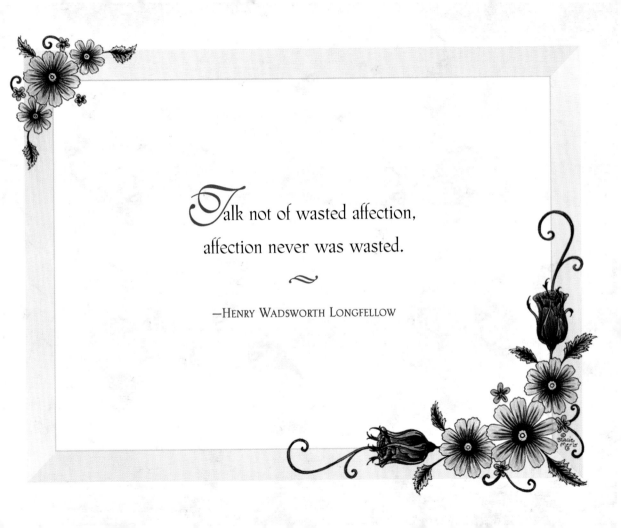

Talk not of wasted affection,
affection never was wasted.

∼

—Henry Wadsworth Longfellow

*L*ove does not
consist in gazing at each
other but in looking together
in the same direction.

—ANTOINE DE SAINT-EXUPÉRY

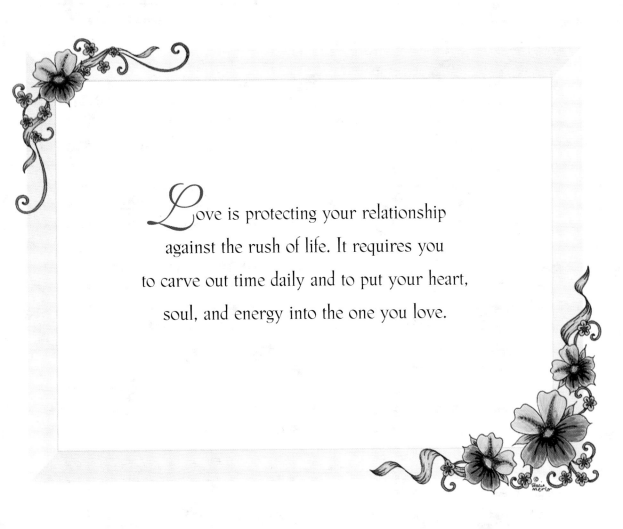

*L*ove is protecting your relationship
against the rush of life. It requires you
to carve out time daily and to put your heart,
soul, and energy into the one you love.

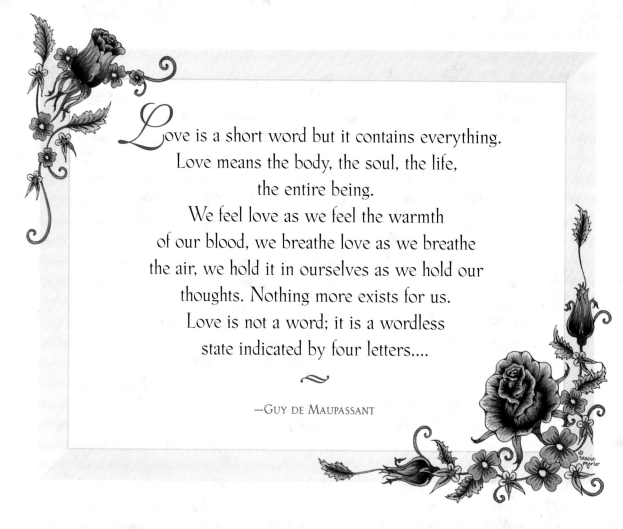

Love is a short word but it contains everything.
Love means the body, the soul, the life,
the entire being.
We feel love as we feel the warmth
of our blood, we breathe love as we breathe
the air, we hold it in ourselves as we hold our
thoughts. Nothing more exists for us.
Love is not a word; it is a wordless
state indicated by four letters....

—GUY DE MAUPASSANT

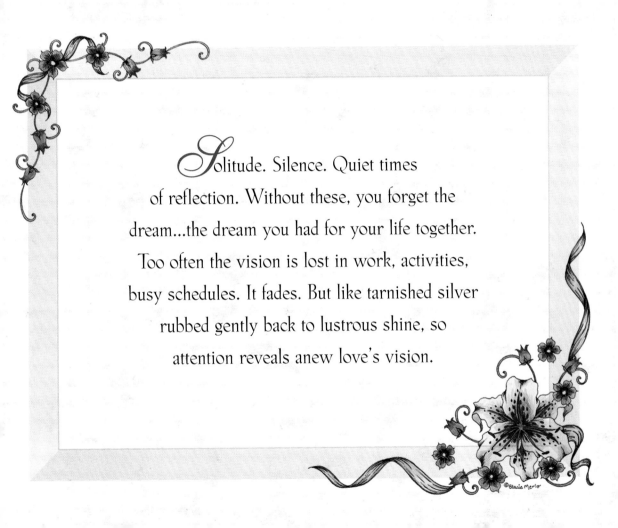

*S*olitude. Silence. Quiet times
of reflection. Without these, you forget the
dream...the dream you had for your life together.
Too often the vision is lost in work, activities,
busy schedules. It fades. But like tarnished silver
rubbed gently back to lustrous shine, so
attention reveals anew love's vision.

*I*t is love in old age, no longer blind,
that is true love. For love's highest intensity
doesn't necessarily mean its highest quality....
Passersby commonly see little beauty in the
embrace of young lovers on a park bench, but the
understanding smile of an old wife to her husband
is one of the loveliest things in the world.

—BOOTH TARKINGTON

Nightfall

I need so much the quiet of your love
After the day's loud strife;
I need your calm all other things above
After the stress of life.
I crave the haven that in your dear heart lies,
After all toil is done,
I need the star shine of your heavenly eyes,
After the day's great sun.

—CHARLES HANSON TOWNE

Come live with me, and be my love,
And we will some new pleasures prove
Of golden sands, and crystal brooks,
With silken lines, and silver hooks.

—JOHN DONNE

*L*ove is, above all,

the gift of oneself.

—Jean Anouilh

CREDITS

Quotes by JoanWinmill Brown and Bill Brown are taken from
Together Each Day by Joan Winmill Brown and Bill Brown, published by
Fleming H. Revell, a division of Baker Book House Co., Grand Rapids, MI,
copyright © 1980. Used by permission.

Quotes from Hugh Prather are taken from *Notes on Love and Courage* by
Hugh Prather, Copyright © 1977 by Hugh Prather. Used by permission of
Doubleday, a division of Bantam Doubleday Dell Publishing Group, Inc.

The quote from Mike Mason is taken from *The Mystery of Marriage*
(Portland, OR: Multnomah Press, 1985).

The quote from David Augsburger is taken from *Sustaining Love*
by David Augsburger, published by Regal Books, Ventura, CA, © 1988.

The quote from Alan Loy McGinnis is taken from *The Romance Factor*,
published by Harper and Row Publishers, Inc., San Francisco, CA, © 1982.

The quote from David L. Leuche is adapted from *The Relationship Manual*
by David L. Leuche, published by the Relationship Institute, Columbia, MD,
© 1981, and quoted in H. Norman Wright, *Finding Your Perfect Mate*
(Eugene, OR: Harvest House Publishers, 1995).

Quotes from Charles Hanson Towne and Anne Campbell are taken from
Poems that Touch the Heart by A. L. Alexander, comp., © 1956.

Stacie Merlo art and calligraphy is offered by FaithWorks
and widely distributed through Isidore Ltd. 1-800-448-0624.

Harvest House Publishers and H. Norman Wright have made
every effort to trace the ownership of all copyrighted poems and obtain
permission for their use. In the event of any question arising from the use
of any poem, we regret any error made and will be pleased to make
the necessary correction in future editions of this book.